Connecting the UK

Cianan Kelly

Front and back cover images

Embraer ERJ-195 and Fokker F-27 images designed in Adobe Photoshop by the author. Corner insert image inspired by a Flybe advertisement using elements from flybe.com.

Title page image

Taken from the author's own collection.

Contents page image

Designed by the author.

Contents

Dedicated to all of the aircraft which no longer serve with Flybe.

The sky is not the same without them.

1. Starting at the end

The first sign that something was wrong came in a form that many enthusiasts have learned to expect. On the 12th of January 2020, the 'Flybe' account on a major social media outlet posted the following message:

"Flybe continues to provide great service and connectivity for our customers while ensuring they can continue to travel as planned. We don't comment on rumour or speculation."

This message, or, at least, a version of it, has appeared on the pages of various airlines just days before their demise.

Unsurprisingly, the next morning, we were told that Flybe was 'on the brink' and that the UK government was being urged to take action. On the 14th, ministers secured a rescue package with the airline's shareholders. IAG (the company which owns British Airways and Aer Lingus, among others) CEO Willie Walsh claimed that the deal was "a blatant misuse of public funds," and accused Virgin, then a Flybe shareholder, of "wanting the taxpayer to pick up the tab for their mismanagement of the airline."

British Airways threatened to file a report with the European Union over what it called 'a breach of state aid rules' that would give Flybe an 'unfair advantage'. Press-hungry Ryanair CEO Michael O'Leary also wrote to the government, reportedly asking them to explain their decision.

Flybe claimed that the government had agreed to defer tax payments of 'under 10 million'. Little more was heard after this, but the airline continued operating normally; it seemed to most of us that the danger had passed. Everything changed on the 4th of March. Reports filtered in from Glasgow that two Q400s had been impounded for non-payment of airport fees. Flights to Aberdeen and Edinburgh departed as planned, but others stayed on the ground, with passengers reporting that crew were 'in tears' and that 'a collapse was imminent'.

The Flybe website, which had previously looked as if nothing was wrong, defaulted to a message which said, "Oops. You might have taken a wrong turn somewhere."

The perfect way to prevent further bookings whilst not making an official announcement, this author noted wryly.

In the early hours of the morning, the announcement came – Flybe was in administration and no flights would be departing. Franchise partner Blue Islands started accepting flat-rate cash payments at airport check-in desks whilst its IT team worked tirelessly behind the scenes to re-establish booking systems – flights had been sold through the Flybe site since 2016. Similar efforts were underway at Eastern Airways, who had also sold flights through Flybe.

Stobart Air, another franchise partner, announced that, unlike the other partners, their flights operated on behalf of Flybe would be cancelled; Aer Lingus Regional-branded services would, however, continue as planned. As with other airline failures, the media went into a feeding frenzy, as did speculators on various aviation forums. Within days, Loganair and Eastern Airways had taken over various Flybe routes, and helped to secure essential connectivity to various airports, including Southampton, Exeter, and many others.

2. The Jersey days

Flybe's history can be traced back to 1979, when the merger of two airlines – Jersey-based Intra Airways and Bournemouth-based Express Air Freight – resulted in the formation of Jersey European Airways. The Intra fleet, consisting of DC-3s, Viscounts, and Heralds, was expanded to include BN-2 Islander, DHC-6 and EMB-110 aircraft; these served various routes from the Channel Islands to the British mainland and various continental destinations.

The main livery at the time consisted of three stripes – two blue, and one red – which ran along the length of the fuselage. Towards the rear of the fuselage the blue lines were interrupted by 'Jersey European' text, after which they continued a short way further. Finally, a stylised JE was situated on the tail of the aircraft.

In 1983, the carrier was purchased by the Walkersteel Group, owners of Blackpool-based Spacegrand. The Jersey European logo was slightly altered, and a new livery was released, which closely followed the Spacegrand colours whilst remaining distinctly separate.

Shorts 360 in the updated livery. (Flybe)

Two bands – black and orange – spanned the length of the fuselage. The underside of the fuselage was painted in a light shade of grey. Some aircraft had a smaller third band, also black, which started at the nose and became progressively smaller for the length of the forward fuselage; however, this was not on all aircraft at the time.

The 'Jersey European' titles were placed beneath the orange band on most aircraft, and they were also featured on the tail, though now mostly lowercase. The EMB-110 aircraft also saw these revised titles on the fuselage, above the windows. A stylized motif from the Jersey coat of arms was also seen on the tail.

A Jersey European Fokker F-27 in the 1993 livery.

In 1991, a third livery was introduced alongside a new logo; this was a simpler, more modern, scheme. The logo featured an arrow made up of five bands of colour, and also formed the main focus of the livery, which was likely introduced to mark the 1993 arrival of new BAe 146 jets.

In 1991, Jersey European operated to 15 destinations, but with only 10 of these being served from Jersey. By 2000, this had increased to 23 destinations: 17 in the UK as well as 6 in continental Europe. Additionally, Jersey European had increased its fleet to 25 aircraft with a further 10 on order – the airline had also moved its base to Exeter, where this story continues.

3. Changing times

In 2000, to better reflect a growing network, Jersey European was rebranded as British European, with a slightly changed logo and livery which stayed recognisable – a key aspect of this ruling was the Air France franchise, which provided around 40% of the company's profit at the time. A company spokesperson stated that the Jersey European name was no longer an accurate reflection of the scope of the carrier's services. Otherwise, operations continued as they had been previously, with British European mainly offering business routes.

During this time, the airline also took delivery of its first Q400 and CRJ aircraft. Whilst the Q400s quickly became the backbone of the fleet alongside the BAe 146, the CRJs proved incompatible with British European's network and were disposed of after less than three years.

In 2002, a further rebranding took place, with British European being shortened to Flybe; this had been the original website address of this airline, with the 'be' standing for British European.

Flybe transformed itself into a low-cost airline, and slowly managed to grow from a niche operator into a well-known brand.

The initial colour scheme saw curved 'Flybe' titles stretching up the tail, with the original 'British European' name in a new FF Blur font featured along the forward fuselage. Below this, and beside the obligatory 'part of Walker Aviation' titles, a coloured band retained some elements of the original brand. The belly of the aircraft was painted 'baby blue', as with the underside of the engine nacelles – these also featured the web address of the airline.

Company photograph of a Q400 in the revised scheme.

This livery was revised shortly afterwards, with the 'British European' titles being downsized and placed beneath the full-sized 'Flybe' name – only one Q400 ever wore the previous livery.

With a new brand, Flybe expanded its reach, opening a variety of low-cost routes from UK airports such as Birmingham, Exeter and Southampton. Though effective on regional services, the existing BAe 146 and Q400 aircraft were not suitable for longer routes to Spanish and Portuguese sun destinations like Málaga and Faro. To solve this problem, Flybe leased a series of Boeing 737-300 aircraft from Astraeus. Though operated by a different airline, all five jets were painted in full Flybe livery; the pilots were from Astraeus, but cabin crew were from BE.

The 737s lasted from 2005 until 2007, by which time Flybe had taken delivery of its first Embraer ERJ-195 from an initial order for 14 such jets. These aircraft, intended to replace the ageing BAe 146 fleet, were deemed by then-CEO Jim French to be the future of the carrier – in 2010, over £1.3bn was spent on an order for up to 140 new Embraer aircraft. This order was mostly cancelled, as the ERJ-195 was deemed too large for a modern Flybe; however, the smaller ERJ-175 was always part of the airline's long-term fleet plans.

In 2006, British Airways announced that it had sold its regional subsidiary BA Connect – the buyer, of course, was Flybe. By March 2007, the purchase was complete, and Flybe had become a business with over £500m in revenue with over 10 million annual passengers. Flybe also inherited the BA Connect fleet – whilst most of the BAe 146 and Dash 8-300 aircraft were phased out relatively quickly, much of the ERJ-145 fleet was retained for Flybe operations until around 2012.

Flybe's expansion continued well into the 2010s, with Jim French outlining plans to start continental hubs – he claimed that the airline's business model had not yet been replicated overseas, meaning that there was a suitable gap in the market. However, losses were mounting, and French stood down in 2013; former easyJet and Air Berlin director Saad Hammad was outlined as his replacement. A period of substantial change was brought upon the airline, which would eventually bring it back to profitability…

4.   Going Scottish: Loganair

In 2007, Loganair faced a dilemma. Its franchise agreement with British Airways, which had lasted for over 20 years, was drawing to a close. The airline had previously been owned by British Midland (BMI), and one possibility, of course, would have been a franchise with Loganair's former parent.

At the same time, Flybe was beginning to emerge as a reputable carrier and, in a move that was tactically intelligent, this was selected as the airline whose brand Loganair was to operate with – unifying English and Scottish regional flying and bringing it under one roof. As with the BA deal, Loganair would retain its own

Air Operator Certificate (AOC) as well as its route network and aircraft, but paint its aircraft in the Flybe colour scheme, sell flights through the Flybe.com website, and adhere to Flybe's pricing structure.

Though Flybe was usually a low-cost operator, and initial fares on Loganair-operated services stayed between £20-50 (depending on the route; according to the 2009 Flybe website), later forum and blog posts suggest that a return trip to Scotland's islands could cost up to £350 in Summer – not exactly cheap!

A notable exception to the franchise was evident in that the Public Service Obligation (PSO) aircraft, used exclusively on government-funded routes, were never painted into Flybe colours; two DHC-6-400 turboprops, operated on island services in a 'Scottish flag' livery – apparently Eastern Airways had also been bidding on the PSO contract to operate the aircraft, so the 'operated by' titles were left unfinished until the service was confirmed as being a Loganair one. The 8-seat Islander aircraft used in Orkney by Loganair remained in a relatively generic scheme with a black underside and small 'Loganair' and 'Orkney Islands Council' titles.

In 2017, ten years after the beginning of the franchise, Loganair opted not to renew the agreement, and thus released a smart new colour scheme featuring a tartan tail inspired by the 'Benyhone' design which had been one of various World Tails liveries used in the days of the British Airways franchise. This would spark competition with Flybe – another story, and another chapter.

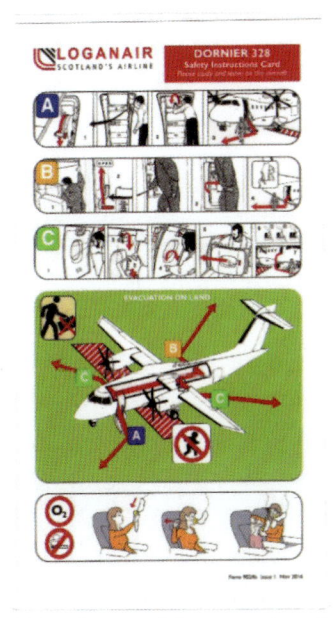

2016 Dornier 328 safety card from an aircraft operated on Flybe's behalf.

5. British European in Finland

An aspect of the business that was not very well-known outside its native region, was the short-lived joint venture between Flybe and Finnair. Logically, it was named Flybe Finland (though it has also been known as Flybe Nordic, it was based in Finland and used the web address Flybe.fi).

The airline was announced in July 2011, with the two carriers arranging a joint purchase of Finncomm Airlines – Flybe would pay €12m, with Finnair paying the remaining €13m of the €25 million total.

Operations began in October 2011, with the originally scheduled date having been pushed back by several months. Most of the Finncomm operations would continue as they had been – the ATR 72-500 turboprops remained, rather than Flybe's regular choice, the Q400 – but the airline would take on the Flybe name and livery, with a small Finnair logo beside the rear boarding door. Aircraft liveries would include a Flybe website address ending in either the standard .com prefix, or the local .fi (Finland) or .ee (Estonia) variants, though the latter pages merely redirected to a version of Flybe.com with the Finnish or Estonian languages, respectively.

A company photograph taken shortly after launch, which includes commercial director Fred 'Tallinn' Kochak, and Mike 'Helsinki' Rutter, MD of Flybe Europe.

The airline closely followed the Flybe experience, with services to over 20 destinations, and a base fare costing €39, according to a promotional map from 2012.

Flybe Finland also operated eleven E190s and two E170s for partner Finnair. One is led to believe that this decision was based on Finnair's preferences rather than those of Flybe, as this would have provided an opportunity to shift its largely loss-making E195 fleet over to another operator. The aircraft did, however, operate in Finnair livery instead of the Flybe scheme; the Finnish carrier had already operated the E190 for several years.

Everything comes to an end eventually, and, in a move that likely aimed to standardise the company, Flybe sold its remaining shares in Flybe Finland to Finnair for the low price of just €1 in late 2014. The deal was confirmed in March 2015, with the airline being rebranded as NORRA (Nordic Regional Airlines) in June of the same year.

In a statement on the company website in 2015, the company's managing director, Maunu Visuri, said:

"Our new name, Nordic Regional Airlines, perfectly describes our company's core business, i.e., regional flying. The northern dimension to the name emphasizes the most important tasks of NORRA's employees – the safe, high-standard and quality production of flight operations for other airline companies, in an agile, environmentally friendly and cost-effective manner. The northern dimension will be presented wonderfully in the commonly used name NORRA, which is a shortening of the company's official name".

6. Purple is the new blue

Under the stewardship of Saad Hammad, Flybe had embarked on a program to shift into profitability. In a Travel Weekly interview, Hammad was quoted as saying that, when he took over, "The airline was in deep trouble. Our cash position was precarious. Our costs were too high, even with the cost-reduction measures already under way. Our commercial capability was weak and too many routes were unprofitable." After selling slots at Gatwick for an estimated £20,000,000, the airline went on to cut 1,100 employees and eliminate a further £47 million of costs. By mid-2014, the carrier had returned to profitability.

The innovative CEO had also decided it was time for a brand refresh. A new logo and set of colours were rolled out on the airline's website and promotional materials from early 2014. The colours, in fact, had been featured in the brand ever since the 'British European' titles beneath the Flybe titles on aircraft, had been replaced with dots, affectionately termed 'lozenges' by staff and enthusiasts alike, the colours of which (yellow, red, and purple) were now featured as the main identity of the brand. As expected, in April 2014, two Q400s were returned from the Brussels Airlines franchise agreement (which is to be explained fully in another chapter), wearing what Flybe's website referred to as a 'commemorative livery'.

This design featured the (now well-known) purple fuselage, wings, and engines, with three diagonally striped bands of yellow, red, and white, towards the rear of the aircraft. Most of the vertical stabilizer was painted in white, with the only rendition of the Flybe logo in its original form filling most of this empty space.

On Q400 and E195 aircraft, the engines featured 'Faster than road or rail' titles. As Loganair's operation mainly saw the purple Saab 340s flying to remote island communities, this phrase was not deemed appropriate, and thus replaced with 'Think in minutes not miles' on the engines of these aircraft. Later, when Eastern Airways began operating for Flybe, their single purple Jetstream 41 did not feature any such slogans; nor did ATR 72s operated by Blue Islands or Stobart Air – this was most likely due to a lack of space on the relatively small engine nacelles.

On the Flybe website, Hammad said, "This is a memorable day for Flybe. Our flagship purple plane reflects our new world of colour and light. Every part of our business has been touched by our brand refresh. Today's flight reflects the start of our exciting new journey as we move to become the UK's local airline of choice with a focus on time-saving and punctual travel for our regional customers."

Company image of a Q400 in the purple scheme.

As most readers will already know, the purple scheme ended up being rolled out across much of the fleet, though, for reasons that have been difficult to fathom, two E195 examples (which were always slated for retirement) were repainted, whereas no E175 aircraft – a type which Flybe was due to continue operating – ever saw the purple scheme.

In 2016, Hammad unexpectedly left the company (a move made through 'mutual consent', and one which saw his salary follow him out) and was replaced by former CityJet CEO, Christine Ourmières-Widener, in early 2017. She embarked on a further program to ensure profitability and introduced another new livery – just four years after the last one was rolled out – which would come at 'no cost' to the carrier.

This livery matched the Close to You brand which had been introduced on everything from adverts to buy-on-board menus. The purple colour was retained, but moved to the rear of the fuselage, with a lilac band separating it from the white forward section. An all-white Flybe logo adorned the tail, with a purple one beside the forward door (notably, the lozenges had been coloured in the same shade of purple; gone were the British European colours, it seemed).

G-JECP showing off the new livery. (Edward Lee)

A little while previously, Flybe CEO Christine Ourmières-Widener had said, "Flybe's strategy is to reduce the fleet size to an optimum level and make the business demand driven rather than capacity-led. Our fleet configuration is an important part of that strategy. We examined exhaustively all the options and concluded the

Bombardier Q400 is the best core aircraft for us. Its superior economy, speed and quietness are ideal for a regional airline such as ourselves. Together with a number of Embraer E175s, our future fleet will be the optimum required for our specific regional route network."

It appeared that Flybe's new livery was to be applied to all such aircraft; the older blue livery was a priority for repainting, as it did not have any evident links to the current brand.

A 'Virgin Connect' concept designed by the author.

In the end, only one aircraft – G-JECP, a Q400, which was in need of a repaint having been involved in a landing accident in Amsterdam – was repainted, as, just months later, the airline was sold to a Virgin-led consortium backed by Cyrus Capital and Stobart Air. This consortium planned to continue Flybe operations, with the Virgin Connect brand being brought into service in mid to late 2020.

7. Franchises galore

As far as Flybe is concerned, there are two types of franchise.

The first of these is a 'white label' franchise, where a Flybe aircraft would operate one of its own aircraft on another airline's behalf. In 1997, the first of these deals was signed, with Jersey European operating BAe 146 aircraft on behalf of Air France from Heathrow to Toulouse and Lyon.

This later grew to include other UK airports such as Birmingham and Glasgow. The deal extended Jersey European's reach, but the franchise was lost in 2004. Various sources suggest that Air France did not want a low-fares airline to be operating its services; Jersey European had, by this point, become Flybe. However, Air France and Flybe continued their relationship, with a codeshare agreement continuing until the latter's demise in 2020.

More recently, Flybe operated four Q400s for Brussels Airlines (SN), primarily on routes to and from the UK.

In March 2012, two aircraft (G-ECOH and G-ECOI) began operating for SN, with the deal extended in June to include two more Q400s – G-ECOK and G-JECY. All four aircraft operated in full Brussels Airlines colours, with 'operated by Flybe' titles on the forward fuselage. Flybe crew would operate the aircraft, and all four would be maintained by Flybe Aviation Services, the carrier's own maintenance provider.

Though not openly announced, all four aircraft had returned to Flybe by 2017, and Brussels Airlines took on Irish operator CityJet; the new agreement was almost identical, aside from the fact that CityJet operated Sukhoi Superjet 100 aircraft in place of Flybe's Q400s. This agreement lasted for only two years, for the

SSJs were plagued with reliability issues from day one. CityJet retired all of these aircraft from its fleet, and Brussels Airlines became to an all-Airbus operator.

Flybe also operated five ATR 72-600 turboprops on behalf of Scandinavian carrier SAS. This airline had retired its own Q400 fleet after a series of landing-gear related accidents took place; SAS contracted Flybe to operate four brand-new ATRs from 2015, with the possibility for two more aircraft if necessary.

The first aircraft, registered as G-FBXA (unmistakably a Flybe machine for that reason alone!), was delivered in September 2015 on lease from Avation plc, and entered service shortly afterwards. All crew were hired by Flybe, and had to speak English and at least one Scandinavian language (required by SAS).

The ATRs were mainly based at Stockholm/Arlanda airport, and any overnight hotel stays in the crew schedule would be managed by Flybe. As with Brussels Airlines, the aircraft wore standard SAS livery with 'operated by Flybe' titles beside the main boarding door. In June 2019, following a Virgin-led consortium's takeover of Flybe, SAS opted to end the franchise; Estonian carrier Nordica (under its

Regional Jet brand) was selected as the new operator.

The second type of franchise agreement involved another airline operating their own services, but on Flybe's behalf. Unlike when Flybe operated for airlines such as SAS, these services would usually be the other carrier's only operation; Flybe, on the other hand, always continued to operate in its own right, at the same time.

The first of these, operators, Loganair, was covered earlier in the book.

In March 2014, Irish carrier Aer Arann signed a franchise agreement with Flybe; they would operate ATR 72s in the purple colour scheme, which had been released at around the same time.

The airline was owned by Stobart Group, and, almost immediately after 'operated by Aer Arann' titles had been applied, its name was changed to Stobart Air and the livery was updated. However, it appears that no announcements were made until after the rebrand, as all articles on the subject make reference only to 'Stobart Air'.

This agreement initially factored in two ATR 72 aircraft and six routes from London Southend; Stobart would fly twice-daily to Rennes and Antwerp, alongside daily services to Münster/Osnabrück, Groningen, Cologne/Bonn and Caen.

Stobart later expanded the Flybe operation to include newer ATR 72-600s. Unlike Loganair, all of whose flights had been operated on behalf of Flybe, Stobart also operated additional services on behalf of Aer Lingus Regional – this model was akin to that of Flybe, with two distinctly separate parts of the business (though it appears that crew were frequently rotated between them; at Flybe, this never happened).

In 2016, another agreement was struck up; this time with Blue Islands, a small operator based in the Channel Islands.

G-ISLK of Blue Islands after the author's journey from Guernsey.

This would see the carrier paint four of its fleet of five ATRs in the striking purple scheme, as Stobart Air had done, and adopt 'BE' flight numbers. Blue Islands would remain an independent operator, with its own aircraft and crew - the onboard experience was also to be very similar to that of Flybe.

Despite initial scepticism around the new lack of competition on some routes, the franchise took off successfully. Apart from the livery and uniform updates, Blue Islands' main operation changed very little – as with the Loganair agreement, the Flybe services were operated on all of the airline's normal routes, rather than specifically contracted ones.

Blue Islands would later retire two of its purple aircraft – G-ISLF and G-ISLI – and replace them with two ATR 72s which operated in an almost all-white livery, save for blue engine nacelles.

G-ISLF, a Blue Islands ATR 42-500. (Edward Lee)

Their other ATR 42, G-ISLH (surprisingly the older of the two, yet the one which remained with the company) had previously worn the pre-franchise livery but was repainted to match the two white ATR 72s. These three aircraft mainly operated the Flybe-branded services but were also suitable for sports charters and other ad-hoc services.

The final franchise partner, Eastern Airways, operated in a similar manner – they operated their original routes and aircraft, but with Flybe flight numbers.

Eastern Airways Saab 2000 (Edward Lee)

Eastern retained their original livery on the majority of their fleet, with small 'Flybe' titles being applied to the forward fuselage. One Jetstream 41 turboprop wore the purple colour scheme, but it was the only aircraft to be repainted.

It was widely speculated that Eastern was to be Flybe's 'replacement' for Loganair, and this was proven to be true after a price war broke out on Scottish islands flights, with Flybe and Eastern in direct competition with Loganair. This did not help Flybe's already parlous financial situation, and, even after the flights had been cut, Flybe posted a loss of £9.4m; Loganair posted similar figures, of which an estimated £6.8m was thought to have resulted from the competition.

Eastern Airways and Blue Islands remained independent, and thus were not affected by the collapse of Flybe; as we saw in the first chapter, they managed to relaunch their own booking systems, and Blue Islands even walked away with the chance to completely reinvent its brand with a smart new livery. Stobart Air cancelled its Flybe-branded services, but will remain an Aer Lingus franchise operator until 2023, when the Irish national carrier intends to hire a new operator.

8.   A second chance

The spectacular demise brought about by mismanagement, overspending, and the beginning of a worldwide epidemic, led many to believe that Flybe's services would not be returning. However, after six Embraer ERJ-175 jets were re-registered with 'Flybe Holdings Cayman Ltd.', enthusiasts began to speculate that all was not as it seemed. Perhaps Flybe was planning a relaunch?

In October 2020, it was revealed that some aspects of these rumours were indeed correct. Thyme Opco, a division of Cyrus Capital (one of the shareholders involved in 'Virgin Connect'), announced that it had purchased various Flybe assets, including the brand name, and, more importantly, spare parts for the Bombardier Q400. More recently, in January 2020, an ex-Austrian Q400 was re-registered as G-CLXC, and now appears to be owned by Thyme Opco. Whilst this book was being written, it emerged that G-CLXC had been flown to Exeter, and now appears to be waiting for a repaint.

Could this be the first 'new' aircraft for Flybe?
Only time will tell...

9.   The personal touch

Since I began writing this book, a lot of people have got in touch with their own experiences of Flybe. This chapter is entirely dedicated to the feedback that I have received.

"A pleasant flight to an original destination, Flybe had the merit of offering frequent and competitively priced flights. It was a regional airline which offers some very interesting, atypical routes. A mix of legacy and low-cost airlines that is becoming the norm. The crew was particularly pleasant and professional." **Dorian, a flight reporter.**

"My experience was flawless from start to finish… Extremely smooth flight… We arrived earlier than expected… Very comfortable and clean interior…polite, helpful staff…" **Emma, who travelled with Flybe to visit family.**

"It was a very nice airline and I enjoyed flying with them many times. Their service was amazing, and I loved flying on the Dash 8. Such a nice aircraft and I think it's very sad that they have left the industry." **Matthew, a planespotter.**

"I've flown with flybe a good 4- or 5-times SOU-MAN, very nice flights actually, the staff were all really good. Had a go around at MAN once due to high crosswinds but the crew handled it very well, came round for a smooth landing the second time, some nice in flight snacks they served too. And I really liked their loyalty system, like we got a discount the third or fourth time due to flying with them before. Overall, lovely airline, shame they had to go into administration like they did." **Sam, a planespotter.**

"Even though I didn't fly with Flybe, the airline was iconic. Their livery was original, the aircraft they used were special. Flybe connected the UK. They also helped connect the UK to Europe. The original airline will be deeply missed, but I, as with many others, am looking forward to the new Flybe." **Oliver, an aviation enthusiast.**

"Some of my fondest family memories were made possible by the Southampton to Newcastle on the Q400. Having family spread all over the country, the chance to spend time together was rare, but Flybe made it happen. When I became seven, I did my first flight as an un - accompanied minor. As one of my first memorable flying experiences, it sparked my interest in aviation and, by the return flight back to Southampton, i was spotting and taking registration numbers. In total, I did eight flights as an unaccompanied minor, and countless more with my family. Now that their operation has ceased, it is certain that Flybe's purple and white Q400's in airports around the UK and Europe will be sorely missed." **Isaac, aviation enthusiast and aircraft model collector.**

"Loved Flybe and their DH8D as the first aircraft and airline I spotted. I started spotting when I was 4 when me and my Nan used to get the train to Southampton and spot all day." **Sam, planespotter**

"The day I realised what a vital and important service Flybe provided to UK regional connectivity was when we were operating an early morning IOM-MAN on behalf of Flybe. I absolutely loved that sector, breaking cloud over the city of Manchester at 8am, the sun rising ahead, the rush hour traffic down below in the dark and ATC carefully slotting us in amongst all of the 'big boys' as they arrived from far flung destinations.

On arrival into Manchester a communication discrepancy between the ground crew and caterers meant that we were delayed in helping a young passenger with reduced mobility disembark the aircraft. I left the flight deck to carry out my external inspection and his eyes lit up when he saw 'the pilot' (I'm the 'assistant pilot' but I wasn't going to let that ruin his day)! Knowing vaguely what had happened I sat down with him and his mother to apologise for the issue, make them feel safe and understood and simply to have a chat. The operation was carrying on around them and from the outside I felt this may have made them feel forgotten or unimportant. They were visiting Manchester for a hospital appointment and this was in fact a very common reason for passengers travelling between the Isle of Man and both Liverpool and Manchester. They were lovely people and really pleased that I'd bothered to take the time to spend some time with them. Soon enough they were on their way and I was back out in the cold making sure our aircraft was safe to go all over again.

This was a vital public service that Flybe provided which I'm saddened to no longer be a part of, but glad that I contributed to making a difference to the lives of a few people along the way." **James, ATR 72-600 First Officer, Stobart Air (Flybe Franchise Partner)**

"It was an absolute pleasure to fly for Flybe; I didn't class the people as colleagues or friends, we were all one big extended family. Every day was different, but you could always rely on the crews for professionalism, integrity and fun! The sky isn't the same without the purple machines (and crew) in it!" **Emily, Q400 Captain, Flybe**

Flybe were like a doorstep airline, serving the more niche airports around the UK and Europe, they felt more personal than the larger airlines like British Airways and Virgin Atlantic.

Their fleet of Q400s was also so iconic, being the largest operator of its kind, flying them at 10,000 to 20,000 feet around the UK meant you could see so much of the UK cityscape and countryside. Flybe was an airline unlike any other. **'Aviation18', YouTuber**

"Flybe was one of those small family-like airlines, where it is not too large to be impersonal.

Almost a sense of community, perhaps it was part of its DNA from its historic background down in Exeter as Jersey European, which I used dispatch from LTN back in the 1990's at the weekend's. It is for certain; it is one that will be sadly missed.

There is something about marshalling a prop aircraft where you are near enough eye level with the flight crew that you don't have with the big jets, especially here at Heathrow. British Aviation is poorer with the loss of this little regional airline." **'Airside Ian'**

"Flybe was the backbone of British travel; it was like a city hopper that went city to city." **Reece, an aviation enthusiast.**
"I went to Paris Charles de Gaulle on Flybe. Lovely service and so incredible how we parked next to a 777 lucky enough to get on the [Scotland] livery [on the Q400]." **Isaac, a planespotter.**

"I think they were great! I always used to love the background sound of the turboprops at Manchester, seeing them taxi on one engine and starting up the other as they neared the runway. I also loved how the pilots always used to wave." **Samuel, an aviation enthusiast.**

Before the pandemic I used to travel very often for work. When I lived in the Midlands I often flew from Birmingham to some very exciting places. Often Flybe would be the first part of my trip, taking me to Amsterdam, before flying off somewhere interesting with KLM. It was always a pleasant, albeit short experience, flying to Amsterdam Schiphol. I was always happy to get the complimentary coffee and sandwich vouchers.
Adam, an international student recruitment officer

"Though the chance to travel with Flybe came relatively infrequently for me, I was always touched by the warm service onboard. My last flight with Flybe, a short 40-minute hop from the Channel Island of Guernsey to Flybe's Southampton base, illustrated this perfectly.

On boarding, passengers were shown to their seats by a member of cabin crew, whilst the other welcomed them onboard. As we taxied out for departure, I noticed that an elderly passenger (likely using the Blue Islands-operated service to travel to a hospital appointment on the mainland) was seated in the exit row, adjacent to a flight attendant's seat. She looked a little worried about this – the stewardess was clearly aware of this and started a short conversation with the passenger. A small thing like that really illustrated the sense of community that you get when travelling with both Flybe and their franchise partners.

In stark contrast to this, on arrival, I saw that almost every stand at Southampton Airport was occupied by a Flybe aircraft; though it may seem like a small company, its reach extended to all corners of the UK." **Author**

Relevant registrations

Information obtained from the planespotters.net database. This is not a comprehensive list - only certain aircraft are included. The information is correct as of February 2021.

SAS ATR 72-600s

G-FBXA (now with Loganair at time of print)
G-FBXB (now with Loganair at time of print)
G-FBXC (now with Stobart Air at time of print
G-FBXD (now with Stobart Air at time of print
G-FBXE (now with Stobart Air at time of print

Brussels Airlines Q400s

G-ECOH (ret. to BE, second to wear purple scheme. Ret. to lessor in March 2020)
G-ECOI (ret. to BE, retained basic Brussels Airlines scheme. Ret. to lessor in March 2020)
G-ECOK (ret. to BE, retained basic Brussels Airlines scheme. Ret. to lessor in March 2020)
G-JECY (ret. BE, first to wear purple scheme. Ret. to lessor in March 2020)

Unusual liveries

Q400

G-JECY (First to wear purple scheme. Fitted with 'Scotland' titles beside L1 door from 2017. Ret. to lessor in March 2020)

G-ECOH (Second to wear purple scheme. Fitted with 'Scotland' titles beside L1 door from 2017. Ret. to lessor in March 2020)

G-JECP (First/only to wear revised purple scheme. Landing gear collapse at AMS in 2017. Ferried to Malta and repainted in 2018. Ret. to lessor in March 2020)

G-JEDP ('Low cost but not at any cost' c/s worn from 2004-2014. Repainted in original purple scheme.)

BAe 146

G-JEBG ('Mansion.com' c/s 2004-2008. Now with Efly at time of print.)

E195

G-FBEJ ('Welcome to Yorkshire' c/s. Ret. to lessor in February 2020)

G-FBEM ('Cancer Research UK - Kids & Teens' c/s. Ret to lessor and leased to Stobart Air 2018-19. Leased to Great Dane Airlines 2019-2020. Now with Bamboo Airways at time of print, leased from Great Dane)

Company photo of the 'Low cost but not at any cost' livery.

Acknowledgements

Many thanks to my family (especially Stigg) for assisting me in the search for suitable references and information.

Extremely valuable documents regarding the history of Jersey European Airways, alongside various other items of memorabilia, were very kindly provided by Nicholas and Esther Sellick – many thanks to both of you.

Most images used within this publication have been sourced from the author's own collection of timetables and other promotional materials. Some exceptions include images and photographs referred to as a 'company image', which have been taken directly from the Flybe media site, which stated that '[the images] may be downloaded from flybe.com and reproduced royalty-free provided full credit is given to the source and to the copyright holder, Flybe.'

All reasonable endeavours have been taken to correctly identify the sources of images, photographs, and quotations in this book. If use has accidentally been made without correct acknowledgement of the originator, please accept my apologies. Should such a situation arise, and I am notified accordingly, I would be pleased to make a suitable amendment for inclusion in any future editions of this book.

Printed in Great Britain
by Amazon